IMAGES OF ENGLAND

Ashton-in-Makerfield and Golborne

The Rt Hon Sir Frederick John Gerard MC, Third Baron Gerard (1883–1953). The Gerards had been Lords of Ashton since the fourteenth century. In 1904, at Lord Gerard's Coming of Age celebrations, all the family were present at a lunch given for 300 cottagers and tenant holders. He was presented with a beautiful smoking cabinet by the men of the Lancashire Hussars. In the evening there was a fireworks display in Garswood Park organised by Messrs. Pain and Souss. In September 1906 Lord Gerard married his cousin Miss Mary Gosselin, daughter of the late Sir Martin and Lady Gosselin of Blakesware, Herts. The ceremony took place at Brompton Oratory in the presence of a large congregation, a troop from the Royal Home Guards being present. Lord Gerard entered the army in 1907 and became a captain two years later. He served in the First World War where he gained a Military Cross but was severely wounded in action. He died in 1953 at his seat Blakesware, near Ware, Hertfordshire, and was interred at Widford, Ware.

IMAGES OF ENGLAND

Ashton-in-Makerfield and Golborne

Tony Ashcroft

NONSUCH

A 1920s postcard showing five local views of Ashton-in-Makerfield.

First published 1997
This new pocket edition 2005
Images unchanged from first edition

Nonsuch Publishing Limited
The Mill, Brimscombe Port,
Stroud, Gloucestershire, GL5 2QG
www.nonsuch-publishing.com

British Library Cataloguing in Publication Data.
A catalogue record for this book is available from the British Library.

ISBN 1-84588-127-3

Typesetting and origination by Nonsuch Publishing Limited
Printed in Great Britain by Oaklands Book Services Limited

Contents

A rare photograph of Italian prisoners at the prisoner-of-war camp which stood on part of the site which is now Byrchall High School, Warrington Road, Ashton-in-Makerfield. During the Second World War the camp held both Italian and German prisoners. One famous ex-prisoner was the Manchester City goalkeeper Bert Trautman, who played in the 1955 Cup Final against Birmingham with a broken neck. He was the first German to have played in a Wembley Cup Final.

A Christmas crib built by some of the Italian prisoners during their 'stay' at the prisoner of war camp, Ashton.

Introduction

The Metropolitan Borough of Wigan, which came into existence on 1 April 1974, was formed by the merger of fourteen former Lancashire local authorities. Two of these areas, Golborne and Ashton-in-Makerfield, form the subject of this book.

Ashton-in-Makerfield (also formerly known as Ashton-le-Willows) is the township with the larger population. The origin of its composite name is a puzzle but possibly stems from 'Ashton' meaning 'ashtown', whilst Makerfield may relate to the word 'Magwyr', a name of Celtic derivation meaning wall or ruin. Another suggestion is 'Macer' meaning a defence or earthwork. Ashton's acreage was 6,249 Qw and population levels rose from 5,679 in 1851 to 18,687 in 1901. The old Urban District comprised the hamlets of Garswood, Downall Green, Pewfall, Bryn and Stubshaw Cross as well as Ashton itself. After the 1974 reorganisation, Pewfall, Garswood and part of Downall Green became part of St Helens Metropolitan Borough, while the rest of the Urban District became part of Wigan Metropolitan Borough.

The Roman road from Wilderspool to Wigan could, until recently, be traced in parts of the township. Before the Norman Conquest, Ashton was part of the Royal Manor of Newton. It was held from at least 1212 by the Brindle family, until most of it was acquired by the Gerards by marriage in about 1350. However, it was not until the sixteenth century, when Sir Thomas Gerard bought the remaining third of the manor from John Atherton, that the family became sole lords. During the Civil War, the Gerards sold their Derby estate to provide money for the Kings' forces. Charles II lodged at Bryn Hall on 15 August 1651 on his way to be defeated at the Battle of Worcester. After the Commonwealth the Gerard family fell into a period of obscurity until the development of coal mining brought wealth back to the family. Then their ancient lineage, Roman Catholicism and new-found wealth enabled them to be on intimate terms with both French and British royalty.

Ashton as we know it really began to develop during the eighteenth and nineteenth centuries with the Industrial Revolution. Coal mining and the growth of the local hinge making industry, together with the opening of factories for spinning and weaving, helped to bring wealth and employment to the area.

Although the Golborne Urban District was formed as an administrative unit in 1894, it was enlarged in 1933 when the townships of Lowton, Kenyon, Culcheth and Glazebury were included. When the 1974 local government reorganisation occurred, the old Urban District was dissolved, part being amalgamated with the Cheshire County District of Warrington whilst the remaining area was transferred to the new Metropolitan Borough of Wigan. For the purposes of this book, the focus of attention has been on the township of Golborne itself, as information about some of the outlying districts can be obtained elsewhere.

As with most settlements, the spelling of Golborne has altered over the centuries, including, Goldeburn (1187), Goldburs (1201), Goldburn (1212), Golburne (1242) and finally Golborne in the sixteenth century. It is thought that the name is of old English origin from 'golde' and 'burna' which means 'stream where marsh marigolds grow'. This may be a reference to Millingford Brook which runs through the township.

Like Ashton, Golborne was included in the Barony of Newton or Makerfield when it was created in about 1200. Also like Ashton, it was included in the parish of Winwick, but unlike Ashton, which had a church in the sixteenth century, it had to wait until 1850 before a church was built there. Up to the middle of the nineteenth century it appears to have been predominantly a small rural community with an area of 6,789 acres. Its recorded population in the 1861 census was a mere 2,776; this rose nearly threefold in 1901 to 6,789.

Although industry was mainly limited to cotton production in the local mills, improvement in transport such as the railways and the spread of industrialisation resulted in mining and engineering being established. This brought with it employment and the prospect of greater prosperity, for some.

The majority of photographs have been taken from Wigan Heritage Services' collection. It is a large collection, built up patiently over the years with most contributions being made by local people anxious to ensure that this specific and valuable part of their local heritage is preserved.

A major problem of compiling a book like this is the lack of thematic variation owing to the limited size of the township as compared to a town or city. Unfortunately not everyone thinks about recording details of the community in which they live and work – until, of course, it is too late to do so. Consequently buildings and events which local people may consider as being unimportant now can, in the future, be very important for the local history researcher. Although a few of the photographs may have appeared elsewhere, it is hoped that most will be new to the majority of readers and that these images, together with the textual information, will encourage people to take more interest in the history of their individual communities.

Farm workers at Charity Farm, Arch Lane, Garswood, *c.* 1900.

One

Aristocracy and Royalty

In March 1898, the Prince of Wales visited Lancashire. During his visit the Prince was the guest of Lord Gerard at Garswood Hall. This formal photograph taken at the Hall includes, from left to right: Col Swanne, Capt Holford, Lady Curzen, Lord Gerard, the Prince of Wales, Sir Kelly Kenny, Gen Brabazon, Lady De Trafford, Lady Gerard, Lady Randolph Churchill, Hon Mrs Oliphant (Lord Gerard's sister), Hon Ethel Gerard, Mr Christopher Sykes and Hon F. Gerard.

An imposing view of Garswood Hall at the turn of the twentieth century. Demolished in 1921, the estate and Hall had been bought by Sir Robert Gerard from the Launder family in the mid-eighteenth century to replace his neighbouring seat at Garswood Old Hall. The Hall was originally built in 1692, but was reconstructed on a much grander scale by Sir John Gerard to a design by John Foster in 1826. Before demolition, the contents of the house were auctioned off by Knight, Frank and Rutley, the sale realising over £9,000 after only six days.

An interior view of Garswood Hall that very few people would have seen. It shows the luxurious nature of Lady Gerard's sitting room at the beginning of the last century.

On 17 March 1906 Lord Gerard officially opened the Carnegie Library at Ashton-in-Makerfield. The building cost £5,843. This venture was made possible through the munificence of the American philanthropist Mr Andrew Carnegie.

On 22 August 1906 the Conservative and Unionist Club at Ashton-in-Makerfield was opened by Lord Gerard, who had also laid the foundation stone in 1905. There was an initial membership of over 200.

Left: Mary, Lady Gerard, was the eldest daughter of Henry Beilby William Milner of Nottingham and granddaughter of the Bishop of Armagh. She was an active social worker and supported the Primrose League in the Newton Division and was also a Patron for Providence Hospital, St Helens. During the First World War she began a VAD Hospital at Garswood Hall funded from her own income. She also helped to establish a local branch of the Red Cross. Lady Gerard died in 1918 after receiving news of the death of a relative at the Battle of Cambrai. She was given a military-style funeral.

Below: At the turn of the twentieth century Lord Gerard was present at the official opening of this private sports pavilion in Ashton-in-Makerfield.

William Cansfield, Second Baron Gerard of Bryn and father of Frederick John, died on 30 July 1902 at Eastwell, his Kentish residence. His body was then brought to Garswood Hall on the Saturday before the funeral. He was buried with full military honours. The cortege left Garswood Hall at 10.30 a.m. and slowly and solemnly made its way down the drive of the park and then onto Warrington Road, before proceeding to the Gerard family vault at St Oswald's Roman Catholic Church. The horses pulling the Royal Artillery gun carriage, which conveyed the coffin draped with the Union Jack, were managed by a number of mounted police. On top of the Union Jack were his sword, medals and busby. The gun carriage itself was painted khaki and attached to a gun of the same colour; a sergeant and five men of the Royal Artillery had charge of it. These groups were behind a number of mounted police and fifty men from the Yeoman Cavalry who marched with arms reversed. Two members of the cavalry can just be seen to the right of the picture. Following the gun carriage was the baronet's charger with top boots reversed, after which came carriages conveying relatives, household staff, estate staff, colliery managers and officials. Finally, there came the main body of Yeomanry who were about three hundred in number. Amongst the wreaths was one from King Edward VII. Besides the main funeral there was a low requiem mass for the soul of Lord Gerard at St James' Church, Spanish Place, London.

To mark the coronation of King George V in June 1911, crowds gathered in Gerard Street, Ashton-in-Makerfield, to view the celebratory processions. At the centre left of the photograph is probably the North Ashton Brass Band which led one of the three sections of the procession to Garswood Hall. The site on which the Union Bank of Manchester Ltd stood is now occupied by Barclays Bank. Coronation beakers were distributed to 4,896 local schoolchildren.

On 10 July 1913, King George V and Queen Mary paid a royal visit to Ashton-in-Makerfield. Here crowds are hoping to catch a glimpse of the royal party as they wait on Warrington Road, near the entrance to Garswood Park, which is behind them. Mr Gilby, headmaster at the Emmanuel British School, who is standing on the road with an umbrella on his arm, is waiting in anticipation.

Two

Local Services

A view from inside the Ashton-in-Makerfield free public library showing the general reading room. Probably taken fairly soon after the opening on 17 March 1906, it shows quite a Spartan interior by today's standards, with long wooden tables and hard backed chairs.

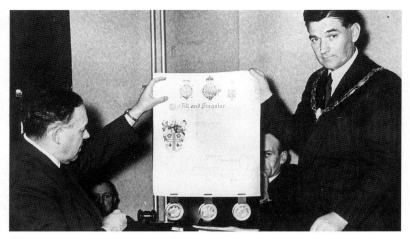

Although the armorial bearings for Golborne Urban District Council were granted on 10 May 1954, they weren't received by the council until 28 October 1954. Here, Cllr W. Naylor, who subscribed the 100 guinea fee for the letters patent from the College of Arms, is presenting the scroll to Cllr J. Armstrong, the council chairman. The motto *Fide et Fiducia* means 'by faith and confidence'.

Civic Sunday, 1951. William Clayton (chairman), together with other members of Golborne Council including Fred Martland (deputy) and Jack Barwell, are on their way to the parish church.

Views of the Ince Water Works at Golborne from a souvenir publication of July 1907. In 1871 the Ince Water Act was passed authorising the Local Board for Ince-in-Makerfield to sink wells and shafts and to make borings for collecting water at Golborne. An aqueduct from the works conveyed the water supply to the Ince district. The works were formally opened on Wednesday 22 May 1872.

On 25 July 1907, a group of members of the Ince District Council, officials and friends made a formal visit to the water works at Golborne. Here they pose in front of their water works. Mr T.M. Percy JP was chairman of the Water Committee.

A view of the largest of the two Jubilee Parks, Wigan Road, Ashton-in-Makerfield, around 1908, showing part of the ornamental lake which has since been filled in. The area now contains tennis courts. The two small parks laid out on the land known as the 'Old Wambs' were handed over to the Urban District Council in July 1897 by Lord Gerard. A wamb was a piece of ill-drained land where water bubbled up.

No municipal park was ever without its public fountain, although the style of each one varied. Here we can see the one erected in the Jubilee Parks, Ashton-in-Makerfield. The figures in the photograph would suggest that it was taken sometime in the early 1900s.

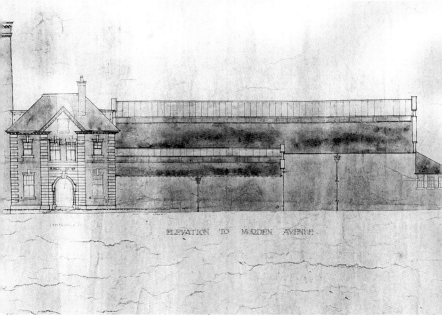

ELEVATION TO MORDEN AVENUE

On 28 February 1910, the newly built public baths at Ashton-in-Makerfield were officially opened by Lady Gerard in the absence of her husband. Leigh architect J.C. Prestwich was responsible for the design of the building, which comprised a plunge bath 91 ft x 46 ft with 43 collapsible dressing boxes around the bath. There were also shower spray baths and two separate clubrooms. When not used for the purposes of swimmers, the plunge bath was covered with a movable floor which converted the room into a public hall, accommodating about 1,000 people. The plan shows the main entrance which was located on Morden Avenue. The building was closed as a public baths in October 1916 because of water leakage and financial problems. However, it remained open as a public hall.

ASHTON
Association,

FOR THE

Prosecution of Felons.

WE the undersigned, being Inhabitants of the Township of ASHTON within MACKERFIELD, in the County of Lancaster, have by Articles agreed to raise and maintain a FUND, to defray the Expences of apprehending and prosecuting to Conviction such Offenders, as shall be found guilty of any Offences against our respective Persons or Properties; And for the more speedy Apprehension of Offenders,

We hereby give Notice,

That Rewards will be paid to the Person or Persons who shall be instrumental in apprehending the Offender or Offenders on his her or their Conviction, according to the Atrociousness of the Offences.

W. Gerard.	James Webster.	Richard Unsworth.
John Whitley.	William Brighouse.	Wilmot Banks.
Roger Adamson.	John Ratcliffe.	John Potter.
Peter Hall.	Thomas Jameson, jun.	Phillip Callon.
William Cunliffe.	James Kitts.	William Bone & Co.
Richard Burchall.	Thomas Pennington.	John Eccles.
James Hope.	Thomas Moss.	Richard Hatton.
James Ashton.	Sarah Berry.	John Shuttleworth.
Peter Polding.	Turner Latham.	James Burchall.
James Speakman.	William Gaskell.	John Marsh.
William Jackson.	William Harris and Son.	John Peet.
Thomas Boardman.	Hugh Whittle.	James Woods.
Hugh Layland.	Thomas Jameson sen.	James Taylor.
Abel Pennington.	James Jameson.	

Rowson & Sons,

Solicitors to the Association.

19th November, 1818.

DUCKER, PRINTER, PRESCOT

A poster, dated 19 November 1818, listing the inhabitants of the township of Asthon-in-Makerfield who agreed to raise a fund to defray the expenses of anyone apprehending and convicting criminals in the township.

Right: Mrs Ellen Tabner (or Taberner), a North Ashton midwife in the early 1900s, lived at 49 Station Road, Garswood. She is seen here in her working dress.

Below: In August 1943 Golborne's new ante-natal clinic was opened at the first aid post in High Street. The clinic, staffed by nurses and midwives, aimed to provide a service to expectant mothers, offering them advice and treatment on alternate Tuesdays. Amongst those attending the opening were: Alderman Robert Barrow (second left), William Heaton (end right) and Nurse Woosey (middle).

On the outbreak of the First World War, Lord Gerard agreed that his residence, Garswood Hall, could become a temporary hospital for wounded soldiers. Here Lady Gerard in a black uniform at the centre poses with a group of nurses, one being a member of the Red Cross.

In July 1921 a group photograph was taken of the workers connected with the Ashton-in-Makerfield Labour Club who had given their time and services to help feed children during a lock out. Over 33,000 meals were provided.

On 3 December 1921, the annual distribution of the Ashton Linen and Woollen Stock Charity took place at St Oswald's Infant School, Ashton-in-Makerfield, to 245 people. Those seen here are part of the group queuing outside the school house door for their charity gift. On this occasion Councillor A. Jones JP (chairman of the district council), Miss Bryden and James Livesey (clerk to the trustees) were amongst the group of trustees of the charity which distributed 28 blankets, 33 shawls, 45 pairs of sheets, 52 lengths of flannel, 21 shirts, 18 quilts, 12 pairs of men's trousers, 13 twills, 9 boy's suits, 4 pairs of boots and shoes, 2 bed ticks, 2 overcoats, 2 under vests, 2 pairs of pants, 1 skirt and 1 cardigan jacket. The charity began with an indenture of 1 August 1588, in which Robert Byrchall gave £14, the interest thereof to be applied in buying shirts and smocks for the poor of Ashton.

In July 1980 the Mayor and Mayoress of Wigan, Cllr and Mrs Charles, together with Annie France, joined residents of Golborne House Sheltered Accommodation, Derby Road, for their 25th Anniversary celebrations. Mrs Constance Smith, who had lived at the home for 14 years, was their Jubilee Queen and can be seen wearing her crown.

A day centre for elderly, handicapped and chronically sick people at Queen Street, Golborne, was opened in October 1981 at a cost of approximately £165,000. From left to right: Mr John Evans MP (who unveiled the plaque), Mrs Evans, Cllr Agnes Peet, Mrs Bridge the mayoress, Cllr Joe Clarke, Mr Jack Barwell and the mayor, Cllr James Bridge. The oldest resident using the centre was ninety-one year-old Mrs Ellen Taylor of Northfield Court, who presented flowers to Mrs Evans and the mayoress.

Part of the cortege at the funeral of Detective Sergeant Josiah Davies who died in a motor accident at Bryn Gates in June 1926. Originally a native of Ulverston, where he joined the county police, he was later stationed at Ashton. Davies was only thirty-six years old at the time of his death.

On 12 November 1932 there was an explosion at the No. 9 Pit of the Edge Green Colliery belonging to the Garswood Hall Colliery Co. of Ashton-in-Makerfield. Gas and roof falls were responsible for the deaths of twenty-five miners out of the hundred who were working down the mine during the night shift. This photograph shows the funeral of two of the victims.

Members of the Golborne 1150 Squadron of the Air Training Corps at their Blackpool camp at Stanley Park East during the early 1940s. Back row, from left to right: R. Black, J. Foy, N. Bannister, J. Lowe, T. Platt, J. Prescott, H. Waring, F. Hallsworth, G. Fenton. Fourth row: J. Cross, S. Blackburn, C. Dunn, J. Simpson, J. Watkins, R. Brindle, J. Dootson, J. Glynn, G. Whelan, S. Taylor. Third row: F. Coleman, E. Jones, N. McMinn, C. Pennington, H. Peters,

R. Chambers, R. Howarth, R. Davies, R. Whitehead, J. Coleman, S. Sargent, A. James. Second row: S. Wolsey, R. Price, J. Marsh, F. Johnson, J. Tickle, J. Parkinson, J. Farrell, C. Carrington, R. Walls, J. Cunliffe, B. Winstanley, J. Rigby. Front row: K. Burrows, T. Rose, J. Casey, E. Waltho, G. Finch, Mr Davies, Mr Bell, camp officer, Mr Bamford, D. Richardson, F. Haslam, T. Smith.

Above: Cadets of 1150 Squadron of the Golborne Air Training Corps in November 1941. The Abram Section can be seen on parade as part of the Abram Warship Week. This section of the squadron was commanded by Flt Lt H.S. Bell and Flg Off H.W. Davies. The Earl of Crawford, who performed the opening ceremony, also inspected the parade. Over two thirds of the £8,000 needed to provide a hull for a defence craft was raised on the opening day.

Left: On 5 September 1848 a regiment of the Lancashire Hussars, raised by Sir John Gerard, was officially gazetted. Formed on Sir John's estate, the troop numbered seventy-five men. Around 1870, this group of Hussars consisting of two privates, two corporals and two sergeants agreed to be photographed.

Public War Memorial, Golborne

The Golborne War Memorial, situated at the Legh Street and Barn Lane corner of the recreation ground, was unveiled in March 1926. Thousands of people gathered near the site and witnessed both the procession and ceremony. Amongst those taking part were members of the War Memorial Committee, over 400 ex-servicemen headed by the Golborne Brass Band and the brass and bugle bands attached to the Prince of Wales Volunteers, Warrington. Mr J. Naylor handed the memorial over to the care of the Council.

Ex-servicemen and women preparing for their annual Remembrance Day Parade at Ashton-in-Makerfield in the mid-1930s.

Ashton Fire Brigade outside the gates of Garswood Hall at the beginning of the twentieth century. The brigade was formed in March 1881 and had fifteen volunteers with a Mr Boardman as their captain. Some of the members seen here are: Fred Odgen (driver), Mr Roberts (standing by the horses), William Sutton, J. Ogden and Mr Williams.

Around 1940 there was an Auxiliary Fire Service attached to Harben's Mill which produced artificial silk. The driver of the AFS vehicle is Stanley Jenkinson, an employee of Naylor Brothers.

Three

House and Home

In 1921 Mr and Mrs Williams, together with their seven children, were evicted from their family home in Bolton Road, Ashton-in-Makerfield.

Above: This is the lodge which belonged to the large house known as The Holme or 'Holmes' off Bridge Street, Golborne, very near the 'Queen Anne'. In 1881, the census recorded that a William Pope (a coachman, born at Thornton-le-Moors) was living here with his wife and two sons. When the census was taken The Holme had no occupants, although in 1891 Peter Edmondson, a colliery proprietor, was in residence with his wife, daughter, two nieces, and four servants.

Left: One of the lodges at Garswood Hall, Ashton-in-Makerfield, c. 1950. The initials 'J.G.' which can be seen on the building are those of the twelfth baronet Sir John Gerard, who made additions to the hall in a Grecian style. This building was later used as estate offices before becoming a private residence.

Drummers House, Drummers Field, Bryn, as seen at the beginning of the last century. The style of the architecture suggests that it was built sometime in the seventeenth century. At one time it was occupied by Mr David Shaw, lock and hinge manufacturer.

Booths Brow Farm, North Ashton, around the turn of the twentieth century.

Number 44 Bridge Street, Golborne, is also known as Holly Cottage. The photograph was probably taken sometime during the early 1900s when the building was covered with ivy. The cottage is still occupied today.

Low Bank Farm, off Low Bank Road, North Ashton, c. 1900.

Dove House Farm – known as 'Eleven Apostles' - was located on Ashton Road, Golborne. The name 'Eleven Apostles' refers to the eleven trees on the right hand side of the road. Originally twelve were planted, but one was struck by lightning.

LANDGATE COTTAGES

PARK LANE BRYN

Landgate Cottages, situated in the Park Lane area of Bryn, c. 1906. 'Landgate' means a long strip of land.

In May 1908 a thunderstorm loomed over Golborne. Lightning during the storm struck a home and shop in Ashton Road causing damage to two large window panes and about 5 sq yds of roof. The estimated cost of the damage was £80. The occupants, Mr and Mrs Kenny and their three children, who were lucky to escape unharmed, view the damage.

Sometime around the mid-1920s these two figures could be seen standing in the doorway of 63 Heath Road, Ashton-in-Makerfield, one of the many terraced properties in the area. They were possibly members of William Wildman's family. Notice the strap-fastening clogs being worn.

Legh Street, Golborne in the early 1900s showing a variety of styles in terraced housing. The chimney in the background was part of Brookside Paper Mill. This was later taken over by the Walpamur Company before becoming the Sunpat Works. In the 1960s Rowntree Mackintosh acquired the property. The Legh Arms Inn can just be seen on the right of the picture. Built in 1869 at a cost of around £700, it hoped to attract young gentlemen 'who indulged in innocent recreation of cricket and ball', because it was adjacent to a public recreation ground. In 1878 the newly renovated Legh Arms opened with Mrs Dean as landlady.

The newly built Heywood Estate in Golborne, around the middle of the 1930s.

Four

Shops and Pubs

Until the retail revolution of the 1960s, small Co-operative stores were a common sight in every town. Park Lane Friendly Co-operative Society had numerous branches throughout Ashton-in-Makerfield.

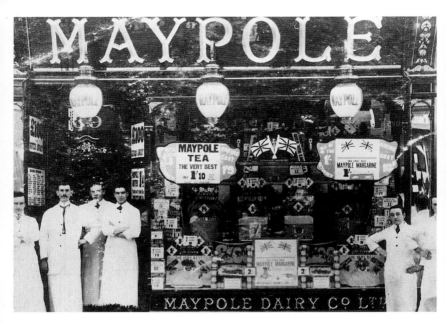

Above: The Maypole Dairy Company had numerous shops such as this one at 12 Gerard Street, Ashton. Note that the shop assistants are all men, and the prices of goods are in old currency.

Left: Charles Grose was listed as an ironmonger of 208 Bolton Road, Ashton-in-Makerfield, in a 1918 trade directory. Here he is outside his shop around this date. Presumably the occupants of the trap are his wife (wearing a white hat) and their two children. The girl standing by the horse may have been another daughter who helped in the store. Notice the row of mugs displayed in the window.

Right: Although George Edward Turner of 44 Gerard Street, Ashton-in-Makerfield, was listed in the local directories during the 1910s as a tea dealer, his main trade was obviously in hardware items. The faded lettering over the shop front window appears to read 'Useful presents to give with all our teas'. The shop window, frontage and balcony are all cluttered with every conceivable object and must have attracted the eye of all passers by.

Below: From the late 1890s until sometime just before 1913, John Beswick owned an ironmongers shop in High Street, Golborne. By 1913 his son Lawrence had taken over the business. Besides selling general hardware items, fishing tackle could also be bought. Note the riddles used by pit-brow lassies for riddling coal and the large, pointed shovels they used for moving loose coal.

Left: Roberts Barrow's grocery shop, 56 High Street, Golborne, around 1910. Barrow was well known in Golborne and the surrounding district. In January 1901 he married Ellen Taylor of Golborne, sister to Henry and Samuel Taylor – famous for their Gold Medal bread. 'Bob' Barrow, as he was known, was a local Methodist preacher and a keen sportsman with a love of cricket.

Below: A typical row of shops at Heath Street, Golborne, in the early part of the century.

Opposite: In the early 1920s, J. Cottom's grocers shop could be found at 205 Bolton Road, Ashton-in-Makerfield, which was at the junction of Bolton Road and Bryn Road. It was a typical corner shop with a wide range of goods from Carnation milk, Fry's chocolate, branflakes and Lux soap to sacks of potatoes.

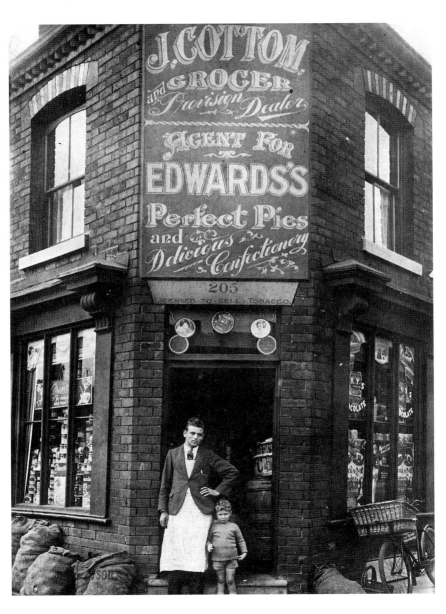

J. Dunn Ltd (confectioners and tobacconists) occupied Rockleigh House, 50 Bolton Road, Ashton-in-Makerfield, from 1950 until 1969. Prior to that the dentist William Aspinall had been in residence. He was a registered dental practitioner in 1891 but had been in practice from July 1878. Around 1969 the building became Rockleigh Guest House which is still in existence today.

Employees of Morris' Dining Rooms pose for the photographer outside their place of work around 1920. Originally the refreshment rooms at 62 Bryn Street, Ashton-in-Makerfield, were run by Morris and Pennington but later became known as Morris' and remained in business from before 1920 until the late 1960s. After this they became the Norweb Electrical Shop.

A photograph of a hairdresser's shop, possibly taken in the 1930s. The property belonged to Harold and Maud Marsh of 59 High Street, Golborne. The previous owner of the business had been Mr C. Penkethman for whom Harold had worked as a lather boy. By 1911 he had bought the business from Penkethman at a time when haircutting was 3d and a shave cost 1d. Harold's wife Maud was also in the business as a ladies' hairdresser. Harold retired from the business in 1965.

John Turton's grocers shop at 1 Wigan Road, Golborne, in the late 1890s. Before this he had a shop in Turton Street. It is interesting to note from the doorway lights that he was licensed to sell tobacco.

BENDIX

Your Family Wash in 30 mins
2/6
OPEN 9 a.m. — 6 p.m.
Daily

Self-Service *Launderette*

You simply put in your wash — up to 9 lbs. dry weight — switch on the Bendix and return in 30 minutes. Here are 2 examples of a Bendix load: No. 1 : 4 single sheets, 2 pillow slips, 3 shirts, 5 collars, 2 towels, 4 table napkins, 1 tablecloth ; and No. 2 : 1 cotton bedspread, 2 large bath towels, 2 cotton vests, 2 cotton pants, 2 overalls, 4 tea towels, 2 cotton blouses.

(BENDIX) THE *Launderette* (SELF SERVICE)

70 GERARD STREET, ASHTON-IN-MAKERFIELD

Above: The Leigh Friendly Co-operative Society's branch at Heath Street, Golborne, was opened in December 1861. However, the picture probably dates from the turn of the century. Note the Reading Room next to the Co-op. Other shops include a shoemakers, a small butchers and a drapers.

Left: This advertisement for the launderette at Ashton-in-Makerfield in 1951 is a reminder that not everyone had the luxury of a washing machine at home.

Opposite: To celebrate the jubilee of the Leigh Friendly Co-operative Society in 1907, this commemorative postcard showing the Golborne branches was produced.

Employees at Heath St Branches

1857

1907

Heath St Branches

The Gerard Arms, 32 Gerard Street, Ashton-in-Makerfield, in the mid 1920s when Richard Hilton was the licensed victualler. The pub was built in 1895 and commemorates the Gerards, who were an old established family in the district. The bicycle on the left at No. 34 belonged to the Misses Latham who were fruiterers. To the right was James Fletcher's shop, a general drapers. Lane and Co. letterpress printers also used this building.

The Manor Arms, 34 Church Street, Golborne. The left downstairs window advertises Oldfield Imperial Stout. Oldfield Brewery Ltd operated from Poolstock Lane, Wigan. In March 1926 Walker Cain Ltd took over the brewery with its ninety public houses, so presumably this was one of those affected by the takeover.

This is what the original Stag Hotel would have looked like around 1900. Built in 1890 and situated at 83 Station Road, one of the early licensed victuallers was a Richard Haydock, who remained there until the early 1900s. By 1909 John Hamill had taken over. It is still in business as a public house today.

Sir Charles Napier was a British military commander who conquered much of what is now Pakistan. Was it a coincidence that the pub had a landlord by the name of Thomas Edwards who had been a colour sergeant in the 7th Fusiliers and had obtained three good conduct badges and several medals? Edwards had been on active service during both the Crimean Campaign and the Indian Mutiny.

Left: The Hingemakers Arms, Heath Street, Ashton-in-Makerfield, which is still in existence as a reminder of a once thriving local trade.

Below: This is thought to be the rear of the Royal Hotel, Bank Street, Golborne, probably around the middle of the last century.

Five

Industry

A scene in Naylor Brothers machine shop at Golborne in the 1950s.

Swim Duncan Elijah (and M.D.) Newton

TAILORS.
Appleton George, Newton common
Appleton Henry
Howard Thomas, Crow lane
Knowles Peter, Crow lane
Pickton William, Wargrave
Potter James, Crow lane
Smith G., Earl's town

WHEELWRIGHTS.
Bagshaw Joseph
Glover Robert

CARRIER.
Warrington and Wigan, T. Pickton, Tuesdays, Thursdays, & Saturdays.

Conveyance from the Railway Station at Newton Bridge, several times a day, Edwd. Griffith, station master

GOLBORNE

Is a parish, township, and considerable village, about 2 miles N. by E. from Newton, and 6 miles N. from Warrington. It was formerly in the parish of Winwick, but was constituted a distinct parish in 1849. The *extensive* Cotton Works of Messrs. Brewis and Company give employment to a great number of the inhabitants, and impart animation to the village. There are also two coal pits in the parish worked by Messrs. Evans and Sons. Thomas Legh, Esq., is the principal owner of the soil and lord of the manor, but Mr. William Travers and a few others have estates here, and its rateable value in 1854 was £5,564 12s. 2d.

The *Church*, dedicated to St. Thomas, is a neat stone edifice in the early English style of architecture, opened in 1849, and the living is a rectory in the patronage of the Earl of Derby, and incumbency of the Rev. C. T. Quirk, M.A. Here are also places of worship belonging to the Independents and Wesleyan Methodists, the former built in 1820. A handsome School, with a residence for the master, has been erected here by Messrs. Brewis & Co., who also contribute liberally to its support. It is also used as a Sunday School, in connection with the parish church. There is also a School endowed with £6 a year, being the interest of £120, the residue of the subscriptions for its erection. The money is invested in the road trustees, who have also the appointment of the master. Golborne Lodge, or Park, formerly the residence of the Legh family, is now occupied by John Catterall, Esq., recently a cotton spinner at Preston. Population in 1801, 962; in 1811, 1111; 1821, 1310; 1851, 1910; and at the present time, about 2000.

GOLBORNE PARISH DIRECTORY.

Post Office, at George Bedgood's. Letters arrive from Warrington, 9 30 a.m.; and are despatched thereto, 5 p.m.

MISCELLANY.

Brewis John & Co., cotton spinners and manufacturers, Golborne mills
Catterall John, Esq., Golborne park
Crowther William, manager, Golborne cotton mills
Kenyon Johnson, accountant, Golborne cotton mills
Lloyd Rees, butcher
Newbould Nathan, Esq.
Palin Geo., colliery agent, Edge Green
Parr Robert, clogmaker
Pimblett John, corn dealer
Portus G. B., surgeon
Quirk Rev. C. T., M.A., rector
Wiswall Abel, brick maker
Worsley Mrs. Jane
Wright Thomas, registrar of births and deaths

CLASSIFICATION OF TRADES.

ACADEMIES AND SCHOOLS.
Endowed School,—T. Wright, mstr.
Golborne School,—T. Milbourn, mstr

BLACKSMITHS.
Birchall G.
Forster William

BOOT AND SHOE MAKERS.
Clayton James
Claxton John

FARMERS.
Bate Thomas
Bent Samuel
Birchall H.
Bridge James
Carter John
Caunce Margaret
Fearns John
Heyes Samuel
Hurst James
Jackson James
Livesley Richard
Moncks Richard
Peters Alice
Pierpoint Elizabeth
Pimblett John W.
Reeves William
Street Joseph
Travers William, (yeoman and grocer)
Wakefield John
Widdows Thomas

GROCERS & DLRS. IN SUNDRIES.
Banks Sarah

Bedgood George
Bithell Ralph
Cook John
Forster Mary
Glover James
Hart Roger
Lawson William
Mitchell Thomas
Partington Ralph, Edge green
Travers William, (and yeoman)
Unsworth Ann
Unsworth John

STONE MASON AND BUILDER.
Ashcroft John

TAILORS.
Marsh John
Proctor Henry
Turner Thomas

TAVERNS.
New Inn, William Wilson
Queen Anne, Margaret Caunce
Red Lion, George Lowe
Victoria, Thomas Crouchley

BEER HOUSES.
Birchall G.
Bithell Ralph
Cunliffe Ann
Mort Samuel
Wright John

LOWTON PARISH.

LOWTON, a parish, township, and chapelry, was under Winwick until 1845, when it was constituted a distinct parish. It contains a village of its own name, 2 miles N.E. from Newton, 3 from Leigh,

Pages from the Mannex trade directory of 1855 for Golborne.

Opposite: A group of pit brow lassies who were working at Park Colliery, Garswood, in the early 1920s.

Park Lane Colliery, Bryn, Ashton-in-Makerfield, around the turn of the century. Colliery wagon No. 1296 is used as a backdrop for these colliery employees and their cat during a rest period.

A group of Garswood Hall Colliery workers outside the main pay office on the colliery site, c. 1900. The office was situated near the war memorial on Wigan Road where the Groundwork Trust now has its office.

In 1904 Herbert Smith received this Lancashire and Cheshire Miners' Federation certificate.

Members of the Ashton miners' rescue team at the beginning of the 1920s.

Opposite above: Pewfall Colliery, situated on the north side of Liverpool Road, Ashton-in-Makerfield, was sunk by Samuel Clough. After Samuel's death the colliery was purchased from the executors by Richard Evans & Co. In 1894 it was estimated that 220 people were employed in the four shafts. This photograph of the pit head was taken in the early part of the century before the closure of the colliery in late 1911, all coal having been worked out.

Opposite below: In April 1989 these three miners share a conversation in the pit baths area of Golborne Colliery.

NOTICE
These Baths
Will be Locked From
9 O'clock till 11.45AM
Each Day

By Order
MANAGER

A view of Golborne Colliery in 1988, just before its closure. The site is now occupied by Golborne Enterprise Park.

Some of the nineteen retired miners from Golborne Colliery in December 1981. Each one received an NCB framed certificate and a miner's lamp for their service to the industry which totalled 749 years. The awards were presented by the colliery manager Mr Barry Chadwick to, from left to right: J. Fitzpatrick (46 years), H. Pownall (46 years), J. Gibney (30 years), F. Mullaney (43 years), F. Owen (47 years), R. Davies (46 years), L. Whitter (40 years), H. Pilling (43 years), J. Bates (38 years), J. Corbett (35 years), J. Birkett (44 years), C. Keenan (46 years), L. Prior (47 years), O. Lodge (17 years), H. Gibbons (35 years), M. Harrison (45 years) J. Damosevicius (30 years), J. Dooney (25 years), R. Partington (46 years).

Opposite: This advertisement from the Leigh Journal of 1965 is a reminder of the time when coal mining was a thriving industry as well as being a major employer. All the mines listed have now closed. However, the surface buildings at Astley Green have been converted into a mining museum.

Come back into
MINING TODAY
and enjoy

PERMANENT EMPLOYMENT AND A SECURE FUTURE

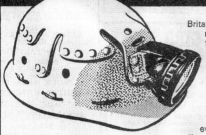

Britain's industries will want coal, millions of tons of it for years to come. So coalmining is an industry with a secure future. Millions of pounds are being spent on new machines. Ex-miners returning to the industry will find changes and improvements everywhere. Conditions are better than ever before. Above all, mining offers you permanent employment high pay and many additional benefits.

VACANCIES NOW FOR EX-MINERS AT THE FOLLOWING COLLIERIES.

Astley Green, Bedford, Bickershaw, Bold, Clockface Golborne, Mosley Common & Parsonage

Apply to your local Employment Exchange or the

**NATIONAL COAL BOARD, West Lancashire Area Headquarters
CLIPSLEY LANE, HAYDOCK, NR. ST. HELENS, or
East Lancashire Area Headquarters, BRIDGEWATER ROAD, WALKDEN**

Issued by the NATIONAL COAL BOARD,
North Western Division, 40 Portland Street, Manchester, 1

972 Ⓚ

Barn Lane in the early part of the last century. From the 1891 census it is known that John Robinson, a mining engineer lived at No. 1. Thomas Halliday, a cotton manufacturer resided at Highfield (No. 3) and Jonathan Heyworth, a cotton mill overlooker was at No. 5. The building in the centre of the picture is Upper Mill, also known as 'The Blacking Mill'. Originally it was a cotton mill until Harrison's Chair Works took it over to produce cinema seats. Later it became a second hand car sales room. At the rear of the mill was Mathers Jam Works. The site is now an industrial estate.

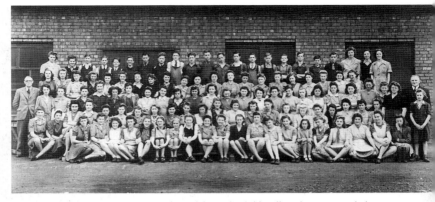

In 1946 this group photograph was taken of the Makerfield Mill workers, many of whom were apprentice weavers.

Browns Mill or Parkside Mill in Golborne has a chequered history. It was built in 1839 as a cotton spinning mill. Production continued until the First World War, when it closed down. However, it reopened later for the production of artificial silk. After 1959 the owners, Courtaulds, transferred production to Coventry, but the mill was bought by Tattons who processed raw yarn there. Afterwards the building was used for the production of Crimplene and finally closed in 1980. It was demolished in 1986.

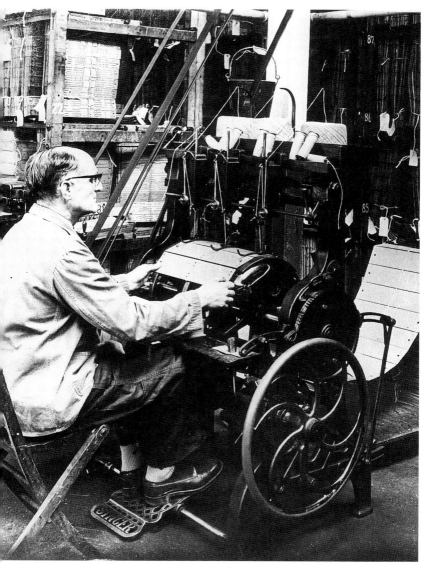

Making punch cards at Makerfield Mill for use at a Jacquard loom, probably in the 1950s.

GOLBORNE URBAN DISTRICT COUNCIL

JUNIOR CLERK (FEMALE)

JUNIOR CLERK (FEMALE required aged 15-16. Salary commencing at £138 per annum and rising annually to a maximum of £380 per annum at age 30 years. Knowledge of shorthand and typewriting would be an advantage. Appointment subject to medical examination and one month's notice on either side.

Application stating age, particulars of education and experience (if any) to reach the undersigned by June 5th, 1954. Canvassing disqualifies. Relationship to any member or enior officer of the Council must be disclosed.

F. MARTLAND,

Clerk of the Council.

COUNCIL OFFICES, LOWTON, NEAR WARRINGTON.

Two advertisements which appeared in the Leigh, Golborne and Hindley Guardian of May 1954 show the type of work prospective employees could find in the area. Under the present Sex Discrimination Act, the Golborne UDC advertisement for a female junior clerk wouldn't be allowed. Note the salary offered. Harbens was a large employer in Golborne.

HARBENS LIMITED

PARKSIDE MILLS. GOLBORNE, WARRINGTON.

Rayon Manufacturers

WELL PAID EMPLOYMENT FOR SELECTED

MEN, WOMEN & GIRLS

Assisted Transport.   Alternating Shifts
Well equipped Welfare and Canteen facilities day and night.

Apply Any Labour Exchange or Direct To Harbens

A view of Thomas Crompton's factory in Ashton-in-Makerfield at the beginning of the 1940s.

A scene at Naylor Brothers' yard in the 1940s. Naylor Brothers of Golborne began as a small family blacksmith business in the late 1890s before expanding and moving their business to Bank Street. Later this firm exported their engineering products to customers worldwide in the mining and power industries. Joseph Naylor, the founder of the firm, died at Southport in 1955 aged 84. His son William Naylor, who took over the company, was made a Freeman of the City of London in 1965. In the mid 1970s, after the firm went into liquidation, Unit Pallets took over the side.

Messrs. Taylor Brothers of Lowton Road, Golborne, were commercial bakers and we see here a view of ovens and two workers, probably around 1910. Like many bakers they frequently competed in bakery competitions. In 1912 for example, they were awarded first prize at both the Worsely Show and Penistone Show for their bread made with Fox yeast which had been supplied by J.H. Hodson, yeast merchant of Wigan. Notice the bakery cat!

Six

On the Road

Golborne Dale, around 1910, when travelling by road was a more leisurely pastime.

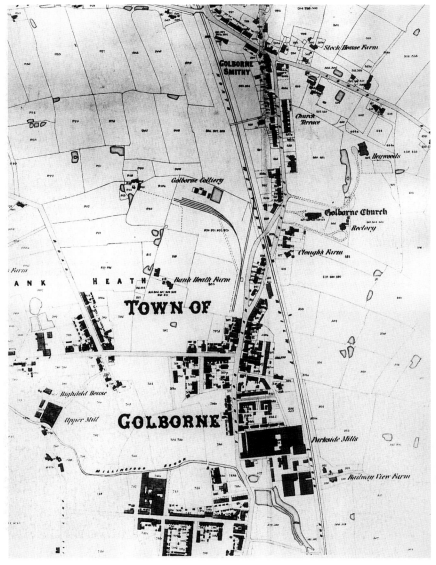

A section from the 1891 Ordnance Survey map which shows part of the township of Golborne.

Roadworks aren't new as this photograph confirms. Taken sometime during the early part of the century, the only thing that has appeared to change is the volume of traffic. The building centre left is the Ram's Head public house which has now been boarded up.

Something of a mystery photograph, this purports to show Bryn Lane – but Bryn Lane ran from Red Gate Farm to Bryn Hall, had no houses on it, and had fallen out of use by the end of the nineteenth century.

Wigan Road, Ashton-in-Makerfield, late 1930s. Notice the old-fashioned set of traffic lights on the pavement (middle left) outside the Emmanuel British School.

Before cars became common, shopkeepers frequently employed delivery boys to take groceries to customers by bicycle. Here one such employee of H.J. Evans, grocer and provision dealer of Station Road, Garswood, poses outside Holy Trinity church. Notice the covered wicker basket in front of the bicycle.

The side of William Barrow's grocers shop in High Street, Golborne, was plastered with advertising posters around 1910, promoting holidays in such places as Cleethorpes, and day excursions (by boat) from Liverpool to the Isle of Man and Llandudno. This is a reminder that although Golborne was inland, the port of Liverpool was relatively near. Were they also trying to encourage people to think about emigrating to Canada? Golborne in the early 1900s also possessed two railway stations, one being called the Great Central, which was opened on 3 January 1900. It was renamed Golborne North on 1 February 1949, and finally closed on 3 February 1952. The railway hoarding is a reminder of the railways' heyday in the locality.

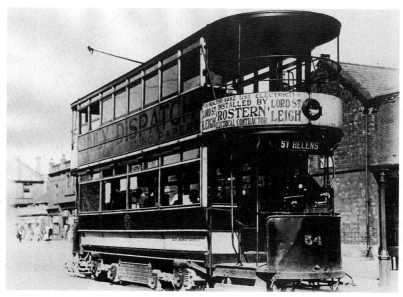

South Lancs tram, No. 54, outside Middleton and Woods in Ashton-in-Makerfield during 1929. Evidently it was a rebuilt Milnes bogie car on its journey to St Helens. It is interesting to note that the company's logo can be seen under the middle of the bottom row windows.

In 1908 this single decker Hurst Nelson tramcar could be seen travelling in Wigan Road, Bryn. Notice the boy in the centre of the photograph who looks as though he is preparing to pick up the horse droppings in the road. Perhaps he intended to sell them to keen gardeners.

This 1907 reproduction of a comic postcard shows the hazards of travelling by tram as perceived by the artist T. Macleod. Last Car would probably be referring to that of a particular day's operation when some passengers were likely to be suffering from 'a few too many'!

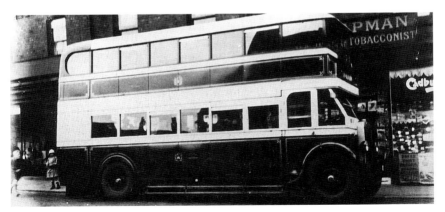

This Wigan Corporation motor bus could be seen in the early 1930s at the bus terminus in Wigan Road, Ashton-in-Makerfield. The Wigan Corporation coat of arms is displayed in the middle of the third and fourth side panels.

In the early 1920s Fred Russell could be seen around Golborne in his horse drawn ice cream cart. However, this was probably only a summer sideline as he is listed in the 1924 trade directory as having a fish and chip shop at No. 2 Lowton Road.

A group from Taylor Brothers in front of their shop at No. 32 Lowton Road, Golborne, around 1890. In Victorian times local deliveries were made by horse drawn vans such as this.

Whilst the Taylor Brothers were delivering their bread by horse-drawn van in Golborne, Joseph Dyke's bakery in Violet Street was providing the same service to customers in Ashton-in-Makerfield in the early 1890s. Note the bread basket being carried by the driver and the difference in style of the van.

By the 1920s Joseph Dyke's Central Bakery at Asthon-in-Makerfield had changed over from horse drawn to horse powered delivery systems.

In the early 1910s, Charles Henry Heyes, a registered coal deliverer, also ran a removal contracting business. Horse-drawn removal vans such as this were designed to be conveyed by flat bed railway wagons if more than a local move was involved.

Delivery vehicles owned by Thomas Crompton & Sons Ltd, hinge and lockmakers of Ashton-in-Makerfield, in the early 1950s. They are parked in York Road alongside the former Record Mill.

Seven

Education

Pupils from St Luke's Curch of England School, Stubshaw Cross, Ashton-in-Makerfield, at the turn of the twentieth century. Built in 1874 it soon became a place of worship and with the increasing numbers, it was thought desirable to have a proper Mission church. On 5 December 1895, the newly erected church was licensed. The curate on the left is possibly Reginald Lane (formerly Wolkenberg).

AT THE COMMITTEE MEETING

OF THE

ASHTON SUNDAY SCHOOLS,

Held at the School Room, Ashton, on Saturday the 7th of July, 1821,

The Rev. JAMES JOHN HORNBY, M. A. Rector of Winwick, in the Chair,

THE FOLLOWING RESOLUTIONS WERE PASSED.

THAT the Thanks of this Meeting be given to the Rev. JAMES JOHN HORNBY, M. A. Rector of Winwick, for his kindness in enabling the Committee to purchase Books, from the Society for Promoting Christian Knowledge, at the reduced Prices.

THAT the Accounts, now read and approved, be published.

THAT the Report, now read, be published.

THAT the Regulations, made at the Establishment of the Schools, be printed.

THAT thirty-four Bibles, and eleven Prayer Books be given to the Assistant Teachers, Monitors, and most deserving Scholars.

THAT Desks, Forms, and Books, be provided for Haydock School, when enlarged.

THAT the Ashton Higher and Lower Schools be enlarged.

THAT the Rev. JAMES J. HORNBY, THOMAS CLAUGHTON, Esq. JOHN WHITLEY, Esq. and the Rev. EDMUND SIBSON, shall be a Committee for the Enlargement of these Schools.

THAT a separate Subscription shall be opened for the especial Purpose of enlarging these Schools; and that a Report of the Receipts, and Expenditure, of this Subscription shall be published.

Mr. ISHERWOOD having resigned the Superintendence of the Seneley Green Sunday Schools, it is unanimously resolved, that the Thanks of this Meeting be given to him for the Ability and Diligence with which he has directed the Seneley Green Schools, since their Institution, in 1813, to the present time.

THAT Mr. JAMES FORSHAW, the Master of the Seneley Green Day School, be appointed to teach the Sunday School in the Seneley Green Lower School, with a Salary of two Shillings a Sunday.

THAT Mr. JAMES STOCK, the Usher in the Day School, in the Ashton Higher School, be appointed to teach the Sunday School in the Seneley Green Higher School, with a Salary of two Shillings a Sunday.

THAT the past Conduct of the other Masters, and of the Mistress, of the Sunday Schools, be approved; and that they be continued at their former Salaries.

THAT a Subscription, for the Support of the Ashton Sunday Schools, be entered into immediately.

THAT the Thanks of this Meeting be given to the Rev. EDMUND SIBSON, and to all the other Friends of this Institution for their Attention to its Interests.

THE Chairman having left the Chair, the Thanks of this Meeting were unanimously voted to the Rev. JAMES JOHN HORNBY, for his able and impartial Conduct, and for his unremitting Attention to the Interests of this large and populous Parish.

REPORT

OF THE

Committee of the Ashton Sunday Schools.

THIS Year twenty-nine Bibles, and sixteen Prayer Books, have been given in your Schools. In all, your Charity has distributed *Two Hundred and Ninety-six Bibles*, and *One Hundred and Forty-one Prayer Books*.

In the following Schedule of the Progress of the Children, you will observe, that from the Alphabet to the Bible, there are seven Classes.

	Ashton Lower School.	Ashton Higher School.	Seneley Green Lower School.	Seneley Green Higher School.	Haydock School.	Total.
The Number of Children whose Names are enrolled in these Schools	287	237	206	200	165	1095
The Number of those Children, that go to a Day School	27	26	30	23	31	137
The Annual Average Number of Children, that attend the Schools	108	105	81	90	71	455
The Number of Children, who, in the Year, 1820, have been advanced only one Class	76	59	58	49	32	274
The Number, that, in the same Time, have been advanced into two Classes	25	18	22	11	9	85
The Number, that, in the same Time, have been advanced three Classes	5	8	6	3	2	24
The Number, that, in the same Time, have been advanced four Classes	0	0	1	0	0	1
The whole Number of Advancements in the Year 1820	141	119	124	80	56	520
The Number of Children who can repeat the School Prayers	90	54	89	63	56	352
The Number of Children, who can repeat the Church Catechism	90	73	89	63	69	384
The Number of Children, who can repeat the Explanation of the Church Catechism	25	32	20	23	20	120

Robert Raikes was a Gloucester-born philanthropist who began the Sunday School movement in 1780. He was encouraged to do so when he saw children wandering in the streets on a Sunday and was determined to teach them to read and repeat the Catechism. From these early beginnings the movement spread all over the country. By 1821, Ashton Sunday Schools had been established. A page from the report of a local committee provides information about the resolutions passed and shows the number of children attending the different schools in the area.

In November 1939, two girls walking their dog in Golborne Dale pass by the Old School House, built around 1697.

Liverpool Road, Ashton-on-Makerfield, possibly in the 1930s, showing St Oswald's Roman Catholic School on the right. In 1846 two buildings were constructed from red sandstone to provide education for the Catholic children. By 1875, a new infant school was established as a separate and official school, which lasted until March 1979 when the school closed. The children moved to the new school in Council Avenue.

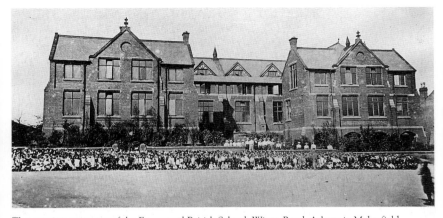

The opening ceremony of the Emmanuel British School, Wigan Road, Ashton-in-Makerfield, took place on 15 May 1893 when there was a large turnout for the occasion. The voluntary school had been erected with funds given by Miss Ruth Evans of Briars Hay, Rainhill. Mr Cubbon of Birkenhead was the architect, Hughes and Stirling of Bootle were the builders, whilst the North Western Educational Company of Liverpool provided the furnishings.

Mr Gilby, headmaster, with staff of the Emmanuel British School, around the time of its official opening in May 1893. He retired on 16 August 1924 after completing over forty years as headmaster and, in 1925, became a magistrate for the Wigan County area. During the First World War he helped raise funds for soldiers at Garswood Hall camp and for the Red Cross Society.

Skitters, a wooded area off Low Bank Road, Ashton-in-Makerfield, was a favourite walking area for generations of Ashtonians. The pit head winding gear in the background is a reminder that coal mining was prevalent in the area. Here a group of children with their teacher in the early 1900s take a rest. The landscape of Skitters was altered after the M6 motorway went through it.

Two lady teachers employed at Our Lady's Roman Catholic School, Bryn, *c.* 1915.

R. W. VALIANT, J.P.

REV. H. SIDDALL.

DR STREET.

MR. R. H. BELL.

MR. C. H. ASTLE,

MR. PETER PENNINGTO

In 1903 these six Ashton-in-Makerfield worthies were school managers of St Thomas' Church of England School, Ashton-in-Makerfield. Mr Peter Pennington was a prominent local builder responsible for the construction of St Thomas' School. His eldest son, John Pennington, went on to build the private residence of Mrs Roosevelt, mother of the American President. Revd Henry Siddall was Vicar of St Thomas' church and the father of seven children. He directed the work to enlarge the old school and initiated plans for a new infant school. In his youth he studied at Cambridge where he took part in the famous Oxford and Cambridge Boat Race. Mr Charles Astle was a local councillor. He had a business as a butcher in Gerard Street and was also vicar's warden. His work in the community made him one of its most popular residents. Mr William Valiant JP was a county magistrate, local manufacturer and sidesman at St Thomas' church. An ardent Conservative, he sat on the District Council and canvassed at local elections. On one occasion it was reported that he threatened to kick the Liberal candidate in 'an unmentionable part of his body'!

Class IV of St Thomas' Church of England School, Ashton-in-Makerfield, around the late 1920s. The conditions appear very basic with long, narrow wooden desks (minus inkwells). Presumably the unsmiling girls are sitting on hard wooden benches. On the brick wall are teaching aids for word associations. However, it appears as though someone had attempted to make it more homely by hanging framed prints. Also notice the two very small vases of flowers on a cabinet against the wall on the left. It is unusual in that the form teacher hasn't been photographed with the children.

A music class at St Thomas' Church of England School, Golborne, probably around the early 1950s.

Eight

Sport and Leisure

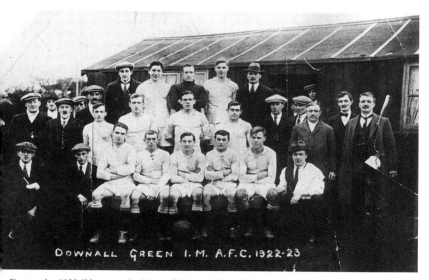

During the 1922/23 season the Downall Green Independent Methodist Association Football Club members found time to pose for the photographer. Before the decline in church attendance in the later part of the twentieth century, almost every church and chapel had its own football team.

A group of ladies from Park Lane Unitarian Chapel during the early part of the century on a day's outing to... Atherton!

In the early 1920s, C.H. Painter & Son were motor engineers and charabanc proprietors with a garage on Wigan Road, Ashton-in-Makerfield. Their premises were situated next to the Robin Hood Hotel. It was one of their charabancs which took this group of Ashton residents to Southport.

In 1932 four generations of the Heyes family from Golborne took a day trip to Blackpool. Here they are photographed in their motor vehicle. The driver was Mr C. Heyes who is seated next to his wife with their granddaughter Dorothy, aged five. In the rear of the car are Dorothy's mother and great grandmother.

'There's a famous seaside place called Blackpool
That's noted for fresh air and fun'.
So went the words of a popular verse. Here a group of Ashton residents pose outside their boarding house in Waterloo Avenue, South Shore.

Other popular seaside resorts, apart from those in Lancashire, were the towns along the coast of North Wales. This group of Welsh residents from Ashton, photographed at Caernarvon Castle, must have felt that they were going home when they visited the area.

Opposite above: Golborne Wesleyan Methodist Church Concert Party and their helpers, *c.* 1921. The 'barrel' line dresses and headbands were the height of fashion. Skirts were still long; short skirts were introduced in 1925.

Opposite below: The work of the Co-operative Society's Women's Guild, which was formed in 1883, always played an important part in the movement. To celebrate the 50th Anniversary of the Park Lane Guild a party was held at Bryn Baptist Chapel in 1933.

In August 1954, members of the Golborne British Legion, together with their wives, prepare to go on their annual outing to Fleetwood. On the table in front of the group, indicated by a white arrow, is 'That Hat', the club's mascot. Soon after this picture was taken the premises had to be vacated and, on 11 April 1955, the new headquarters were opened on Charles Street, Golborne. The ceremony was performed by Brigadier L.C. Mandelberg CBE, DSO, MC, TD.

The North Ashton Village Club was established in 1889 to afford its members 'amusement, improvement and recreation'. As the club had its own bowling green, one of the pursuits it offered was bowling. This photograph of the club's successful team was taken at a much later date, probably around the early 1920s. The staid, formal grouping is made a touch humorous by the person sitting second left in the front row, who seems out of place with his striped socks.

Golborne, like any other English village, had its own cricket team. Here the members pose in their playing attire outside the club house at the Barn Lane ground, probably in the early 1890s. John Brewis, head of the firm of Samuel Brewis & Co., cotton spinners, helped to establish the club and acquire the land needed on which to play.

Park Lane Sunday School Association football team at the end of their successful 1920/21 season. In June 1921 an annual party was given when medals were presented. This event took place in the Shaw Memorial Schools. Peter Gorton presented three sets of medals – two sets to the first team and one to the reserve team. Presentations were also made to Mr H. Molyneux (general secretary), Mr J. Lomax (treasurer) and Mr A. Hand (financial secretary). The president of the club was the Revd J.W. Shaw MA, seen here seated third from the left in the second row.

A group photograph of the bronze medallists from the Ashton-in-Makerfield life-saving class in 1912.

In 1950 Park Lane chapel and schools tennis team became champions of the Wigan Tennis League, beating Keystone, Bickershaw, Roburite, Springfield and central Wigan on the way. Here they proudly sit behind the table which shows off their trophies.

Golborne County Secondary School netball team face the camera during their 1951/52 season.

In August 1981, Golborne Sports and Social Club held a presentation night when awards gained during the sports festival were on show before being handed over to the appropriate winners.

The Three Sisters Recreation Area is a 120 acre site near Bryn Road, Ashton-in-Makerfield. Once a busy mining area, it gained its name from the three slag heaps once found on the site. It was transformed in 1975 to accommodate a wide range of leisure interests including motorcycle sports. This photograph from the early 1980s shows one of the popular motorcycle races.

Nine

Entertainment

The Ashton Ladies Choir at a concert given in the Herman Welsh Chapel, Stubshaw Cross, Ashton-in-Makerfield, c. 1940.

Brass bands were a very popular form of entertainment in the district. In July 1898 the Band of the Lancashire Hussars Yeomanry Cavalry celebrated their Jubilee. In commemoration of the event this group photograph was taken. The bandmaster at this time was Mr Thomas Batley.

Garswood Hall Institute Band, *c.* late 1890s.

Golborne Subscription Band in the mid 1950s, probably outside the Royal Hotel, Bank Street, where they practised. The band was originally formed in the 1920s with Stanley Jennings as conductor. The Ladies Committee helped raise the £300 needed to purchase the uniforms. The band broke up during the Second World War, but reformed later.

Members of the North Ashton Brass Band pose in front of the Holy Trinity Church banners in readiness for the 1931 Procession of Witness. The band was formed in the late 1880s by Mr W. Lowe (band master), Mr P. Greenall, Mr R. Greenall and Mr J. Fairhurst (hon. sec.). In 1933 these four individuals had clocked up a total of approximately 150 years with the band.

JUBILEE | PAVILION

GOLBORNE— | **GOLBORNE—**

[M]on., Tues. Wed Dec 21—23	Mon., Tues. Wed Dec 21—23
[W]alt Disney Full Length Film	John Mills, Elizabeth Sellar
	"THE GENTLE GUNMAN"
"CINDERELLA"	
IN TECHINCOLOR	Thurs. & Sat. 24th—26th. Dec
	Johnny Weissmuller, and
[T]hurs. & Sat. 24th—26th. Dec.	Angela Stevens
	"SAVAGE MUTINY"
[A]nna Maria. Lauritz Melchoir	**Also "Apache Country"**
THE STARS ARE SINGING"	
IN TECHNICOLOR	Sat Mat. 'Songs and Saddles
	'Adventure of Tarzan' Ep 9

An advertisement in the Leigh, Golborne and Hindley Guardian of 18 December 1953 for the Jubilee and Pavilion cinemas at Golborne. The Pavilion, situated in Tanners Lane, opened in the 1920s and finally closed its doors in February 1959 after the second house performance of Fort Dobbs. This slow action western starred Clint Walker in his movie debut. Other members of the cast included Virginia Mayo and Russ Conway. The manager at the time was Mr Walter Potter.

Opposite above: The Palace cinema, Bryn Street, Ashton-in-Makerfield, gaily decorated in May 1937 to celebrate King George VI's coronation. East Meets West was a 1936 British picture starring George Arliss and Godfrey Tearle, whilst The Texas Rangers was an American cowboy film which featured Fred MacMurray, Jack Oakie and Jean Parker.

Opposite below: The Palace, Bryn Street, Ashton-in-Makerfield, finally closed as a cinema on 2 April 1966. Here part of the building is being demolished in order that renovation works can convert it into a shopping arcade.

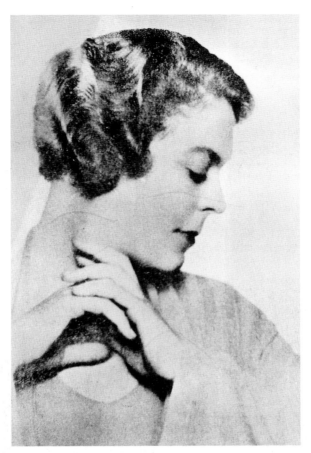

Dame Eva Turner (1892–1990). This Oldham-born soprano was mainly associated with the operatic roles of Verdi and Wagner and is probably one of the finest dramatic sopranos produced by Britain because of her great range and power. She was a distinguished teacher whose pupils included Rita Hunter and Amy Stuart. Although internationally famous, she refused to change her name for the stage. Her father was a native of Standish but at a later date moved to Ashton-on-Makerfield. It was here in October 1934 that Eva sang with the Ashton Choral Society at their concert, which was held in the public baths' hall. She spent some years at the Royal Academy of Music before joining the Carl Rosa Opera Company. She eventually became prima donna of the company and remained with it until 1924 when she appeared at *La Scala*, Milan, with Toscanini. After that success was assured. By 1962 she had been made a DBE. On Eva's death in 1990 her ashes were brought from London to Standish churchyard so that she could be buried with her parents.

Ten

Carnivals and Parades

A horse belonging to Charles Jenkinson of Bank Heath Farm, Golborne, in the 1920s, is ready for the annual May Queen celebrations.

A group of children on a cart with plough and horse, prepare to take part in the annual Golborne May Day celebrations during the 1920s.

Dressed up and raring to go. These revellers' prepared to take part in the Golborne May Day celebrations during the 1930s. Note the large number of horse brasses hanging from the harness on the right.

In July 1913 a children's athletic festival and fete was held in the grounds of Garswood Park as part of the celebrations to mark a royal visit. The proceeds from the event went towards the District Nursing Fund and the Teachers Benevolent and Orphan Fund. As part of the procession was this tableau entitled King Edward rowed up the Dee.

North Ashton residents make the final preparations for the annual Rose Queen ceremony in the early part of this century. The very first Ashton Rose Queen was a Miss Bridge, who was crowned in 1889.

Opposite above: Robert Barrow, wholesale fruit and potato merchant of Golborne, allowed his lorry to be decorated in the early 1950s as part of the annual May Queen festivities.

Opposite below: After having been crowned, a rather stern-looking North Ashton Rose Queen sits for a formal photograph of the event surrounded by her 'loyal subjects', probably sometime before 1914.

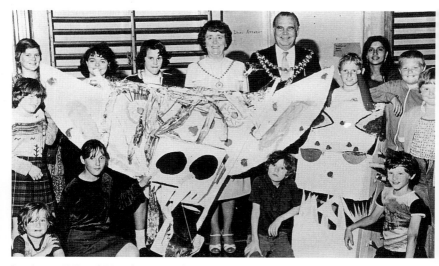

It is August 1981 and Wigan's mayor and mayoress, Cllr and Mrs Jim Bridge, are photographed with children attending a play scheme at Golborne Comprehensive School. The children are seen with part of a giant dragon which featured in the Golborne and Lowton Town medieval display.

In August 1981 there was a medieval flavour to the Golborne and Lowton Town Show. The procession wound its way through Golborne to Turton Street Junior School where a special medieval 'It's a Knockout' competition was staged. The centrepiece of the activities was a replica of a castle designed by the Manchester Arts Workshop. Nearly £1,000 was raised to help buy a minibus for local organisations.

Eleven

Churches and Chapels

An interior view of All Saints' Roman Catholic church at Golborne, which was formally consecrated on Sunday 20 May 1928 by Bishop Dobson of Liverpool. At the afternoon service he confirmed over 200 members of the church. Messrs. Higson and Barker of Bolton were the architects, whilst Mr Fred Whelan of Golborne was responsible for the interior decoration.

The Act of Toleration, passed in 1689, allowed Noncomformists to worship freely, and chapels began to be built, such as this one in Park Lane, erected in 1697. Alterations were made to the building, including the addition of the porch at the left of the picture, in 1871.

Park Lane Unitarian Chapel was noted for its closely-knit congregation of long-established middle class families. This photograph of ladies from the congregation, taken in 1864, communicates a feeling of affluence and likemindedness.

Members of the Women's League at Park Lane Unitarian Chapel in front of the new lych gate. The League raised the £120 necessary for its erection. The gate acted as a memorial to the late Revd Matthew Watkins, a former minister. The opening ceremony was performed by Nurse Leyland of Lower St Stephen Street, Wigan, who had been a regular chapel attender for over seventy years. Originally a lych gate was a roofed gateway to the entrance to a churchyard through which the coffin was carried. It contained seats for the bearers and shelter for those taking part in the service. The word is derived from the Anglo Saxon 'lich', meaning corpse.

A view of St Thomas' old church in Ashton-in-Makerfield, probably around the mid-nineteenth century. There had been chapel on the site since 1577 as Saxton had recorded it on his map of Lancashire. The chapel was rebuilt in 1714, but by 1815 it had become too small for the growing congregation. A vestry meeting was held early in 1815 when it was decided that the structure of the building could be enlarged. The new structure was used until it was rebuilt in 1893.

St Thomas' church, Ashton-in-Makerfield, 1988. The original graveyard has been cleared and relaid as a Garden of Rest. A feature of the tower is the clock dated 15 May 1812, which had been taken from the old church.

Right: Alan Greenwell obtained his MA at University College, Durham, in 1848. A year later he took up his first clerical position as the first Rector of St Thomas', the parish church at Golborne. He remained as rector for five years before becoming chaplain at Durham Gaol. In 1865 he became incumbent at St James the Great, Haydock, where he remained for four years. It was during this period that this photographic portrait was taken. Later he went to live in Bristol where he died, probably sometime before 1915.

Below: A view of the extensive rectory garden at Holy Trinity church, North Ashton, in 1906. The gardener in the centre must have spent some considerable time in mowing the lawn. The rectory itself was built soon after the church in 1837, and although it was impressive and commodious, it became very expensive to maintain. A new rectory was built in 1984.

THE RECTORY
ASHTON.

In December 1882, the Cave-Browne Protestant Institute was officially opened. Situated in Heath Street, Ashton-in-Makerfield, it was a two-storey building consisting of two classrooms, a committee room and other smaller rooms. The cost was approximately £1,000. The Institute was formed when a branch of the Church Association consisting of working men, expressed growing dissatisfaction with the innovations and proceedings of the vicar of the parish, 'especially in his bringing into the parish, despite earnest protests, a clergyman well known as a high churchman'. This occurred in July 1877. When the society tried to influence local opinion by holding lectures on the church premises, the members involved were told by the vicar that they were not wanted in either his choir or Sunday School. The committee therefore contracted for a plot of land and buildings formerly used in connection with the gasworks. An appeal was made and a Miss Cave-Browne from the Midlands subscribed £150. It is after her that the building was named. The Penny Savings Bank was connected with the Institute, as was a Protestant and Evangelical lending library.

Opposite above: In July 1899 the Church Association Sunday School, Ashton-in-Makerfield, held their 21st Anniversary tea party. The banner in the centre of the picture was painted by William Tutill of City Road, London. Made of pure silk, it was blue with an orange border. The floral embellishments and tassels were blue and white. The centre of the panel on one side contained a representation of the school with the words 'Church Association Sunday School, Ashton-in-Makerfield, established 1878'. On the other side was a representation of a crown and sceptre with an open Bible resting on a cushion, above being the words 'My word is truth'. The carrying poles were made of lance wood with brass spear heads.

Opposite below: On 26 June 1932, the newly formed 1st Bryn Company of the Boy's Brigade, St Peter's Church, was presented with their new flag by Revd T.H. Warne (vicar and Company chaplain). In command of the Company was Captain John Moss. This photograph, taken in St Peter's Church schoolyard shows some of the founder members of the brigade. Front row, from left to right: second, Ellis Jolley, fourth, Tom Lowe, fifth, Arthur Winstanley. Second row: third, Thomas Meadows, fourth, Norman Cunliffe. The four boys wearing stiff collars and bow ties were also choir boys at St Peter's church.

Children from All Saints Roman Catholic church, Golborne, parade along High Street in the early 1930s during their Procession of Witness, whilst crowds line the street.

This annual Procession of Witness or 'Walking Day' as it was known, was originally held on the Monday following Trinity Sunday, with a field treat the following Sunday. Later, however, the actual 'Walking Day' was changed to the Sunday itself. This photograph was taken during a service at the end of the walk in the early 1950s when members of Holy Trinity Church congregated on the green at the bottom of Rectory Road. Notice the two large banners which were carried during the procession.

In December 1906, the Carmel Welsh Wesleyan Chapel, Bolton Road, Ashton-in-Makerfield, was officially opened by Revd T. Hughes of Liverpool. Erected at a cost of £700, it had a seating capacity of 300. The group seen here are some of the founder members of the chapel.

A group of children from Carmel Welsh Chapel, Bolton Road, Ashton-in-Makerfield, in 1927, on the occasion of the chapel's Band of Hope Concert Party.

One of the big social movements in the nineteenth century was the Temperance Movement. Disputes arose over whether total abstinence or moderation was the best way of tackling the problem of drunkenness and poverty. There were many different groups trying to change drinking habits. Among these were the Bands of Hope, which were mainly attached to nonconformist chapels. Any person who attended one of the many meetings and publicly decided to abstain from alcoholic drink was given a certificate. This one, dated 17 March 1873, belonged to a Richard Ascroft of Park Lane Chapel.

A group of ladies from one of the Ashton-in-Makerfield branches of the British Women's Temperance Association, probably outside the Manse on Old Road where Henry Wilson, the Congregational minister, his wife Sylvia and their children lived. Sylvia Wilson was an ardent supporter of the Temperance Movement, and after leaving Ashton, became president of the Blackpool branch.

Members of the Golborne Heath Street Wesleyan Church choir, c. 1910.

A wedding group outside Ashton-in-Makerfield Congregational Church, c. 1910.

Left: Edmund Arrowsmith was a Jesuit who was hung, drawn and quartered for his faith at Lancaster in 1628. His right hand was taken to Ashton, where it was preserved by local Catholics. Miracles of healing have been attributed to it from the early eighteenth century. It is now kept at St Oswald's church. Father Arrowsmith was canonized in 1970 by Pope Paul VI.

Below: On 29 August 1959, Golborne Parish Church's new £15,000 assembly hall and extensions were opened by the Rt Revd Clifford Arthur Martin, Bishop of Liverpool (standing). Also in attendance were Revd Newby of Lowton St Mary's Church (seated left on stage) and Rector Arthur Clague of Golborne St Thomas', seated to the right of the bishop, together with former rectors Revd M.H. Gaskell and Archdeacon A. White.

In 1901 the Evangelization Society of Liverpool and London held one of their meetings at Golborne. It appears to have attracted a large crowd of all ages, although the number of women appears to outweigh the number of men.

In October 1913 a van mission, in connection with the British and Foreign Unitarian Association, was held in the Market Place at Ashton-in-Makerfield. Revd H. Fisher Short, who was a resident minister at Park Lane chapel, was the special missioner. The wording on the side reads 'Unitarian Van advocating Truth, Liberty and Religion'.

Here the Revd Matthew Henry Gaskell, Rector of St Thomas' Parish Church, Golborne, around 1945, can be seen with a novel way of advertising a series of sermons to be given at the local church school. With a sandwich board he brings the message to the public by walking the Golborne streets, which obviously causes some amusement.

Twelve

Personalities

John Jonas Kilshaw (1848–1919) was commonly known to the people of Ashton-in-Makerfield as the hermit of Ashton Heath, although he occasionally called himself the Gypsy King. His residence, a hut 3ft high, was built in a ditch situated on Ashton Heath near Haydock Racecourse. It was no more than a dugout, roofed with flags, stones and sack cloth, with an old bucket as a chimney. He washed in a ditch and cut his own hair and beard with a pair of borrowed scissors. Every summer he used to walk to Kent and back to pick strawberries. In September 1919, Kilshaw's body was found on a colliery dirt tip at the Park Lane Collieries. An inquest at the Robin Hood Hotel recorded a verdict of 'death from misadventure'. Most probably he had become intoxicated and had gone to sleep on the tip and been overcome by fumes.

Dora Greenwell (1821–1881), a devotional writer, was the daughter of Thomas Greenwell of Greenwell Ford, near Lanchester, Co. Durham. In 1850 she moved with her father and mother to Golborne, where she stayed for four years with her brother Alan, who was the first Rector of Golborne Parish Church. One person described her as being 'tall, very slender with a gently hesitating manner and soft cooing voice. Eyes not black, but dark, luminous brown and wonderfully vivacious'. Her first volume of poetry was published in 1848. Other writings include: *Carmina Crucis* (1869), *On the Education of an Imbecile* (1869) and *Camera Obscura* (1876). *The Patience of Hope* was praised by the American poet John Greenleaf Whittier for it singular beauty of style. She formed friendships with Christina Rossetti and Josephine Butler. Dora was a well known hymn writer. One of her best known works begins:

'I am not skilled to understand
What God hath willed, what God hath planned;
I only know at His right hand
Stands one who is my Saviour.'

Her eldest brother was William Greenwell, archaeologist and minor canon at Durham Cathedral. He was also a Fellow of the Royal Academy and a Vice President of Archaeologia Aeliana.

John Edward Young (standing second left) lived in Golborne. He served with the 6th Battalion South Lancashire Regiment and saw action in Africa during the Boer War. He and his friends are seen here around the beginning of the twentieth century. After leaving the army he found employment at Golborne Colliery.

Simon Stubbs Brown OBE, JP died at his residence, 2 Regent Road, Birkdale, in November 1924. He was a native of Warwickshire but came to the Wigan district as a young man to assist his uncle William Brown, founder of the firm Messrs. Brown and Nephews, cotton spinners of Worsley Mesnes and Poolstock. He also began to take part in the public life of the community. For some years he had been a prominent member of the Pemberton Local Board. Later he moved to Golborne where the firm worked Parkside Mills and eventually became the first Chairman of Golborne District Council from 1894 until 1902. Whilst at Golborne he resided at Sunny Bank before returning to Wigan, and eventually retiring to Southport. He was one of the oldest members of Lancashire County Council, having been elected in 1888. He had also been a County Magistrate and was Past Master of the Wigan Lodge of Free Masons. For his work associated with converting Winwick Asylum into a military hospital during the First World War he received the OBE. Brown's will indicates that he left a gross estate to the value of £57,084 0s 2d with net personalty of £56,717 12s 1d.

The Eight Lancashire Lads, a famous clog dancing troupe, originated in Golborne. In the mid-1890s John Willie Jackson, a white lead worker, assisted by his school teacher wife entered his five children in a talent contest at Blackpool, which they won easily. From this they were offered an engagement at Blackpool's Central Pier. Three other children were brought from Golborne to bring the total to eight. The original members of the troupe included: John Willie Jackson, jnr., Herbert, Alfred Stephen and sister Rosie (hair cut short to make her look like a boy), George, Jim and Billy Cawley. After a run at Blackpool they worked the halls and finally appeared in London. At Canterbury one of the twins fell ill and a young Charlie Chaplin took his place. It is reputed that George Cawley gave Chaplin dancing lessons in Golborne station waiting room. Many famous personalities associated with the Lads included, Jack Edge, Tommy Handley and Nat Jackley.

Stephen Walsh (1859–1929) trade union leader and politician, was born in Liverpool. At about the age of thirteen he began work as a miner at Ashton-in-Makerfield. By 1901 Walsh had become an agent for the Lancashire and Cheshire Miners' Federation, subsequently becoming its president. In 1922 he was made Vice President of the Miners' Federation of Great Britain. His political career began when he contested and won the election as Labour candidate for the Ince Division in 1906, a seat he held until his death. During his political career he was Parliamentary Secretary to the Ministry of National Service in 1917 and from 1914 to 1920 was chairman of the miners' section of the English Conciliation Board. On the formation of the first Labour Government in 1924, Walsh was appointed Secretary of State for War and President of the Army Council. Whilst Secretary of State, Walsh visited Aldershot in 1924 where he met the King and Queen as the photograph records. In 1885 he had married Anne Adamson, daughter of a Lancashire miner. Their eldest son Arthur was awarded the Military Cross, but died in action in 1918.

Peter Kane (1918–1991) was born in Heywood between Rochdale and Bury. Whilst still a baby his parents moved to Golborne, which remained his home. Peter's name was Cain but the Boxing Board of Control misspelt this on the registration form. However, he decided to retain the incorrect spelling for good luck. Starting off in a fairground boxing booth he finally became World Flyweight Champion between 1938 and 1943, and European Bantamweight Champion from 1947 to 1948. To achieve this he fought in 108 contests, winning 98 and losing 7. For the flyweight championships in 1938 he outpounded the American Jackie Jurich, but did not defend the title until 1943, when Jackie Paterson knocked him out in 61 seconds. In September 1947 he beat Theo Medina to take the European title, which he lost to Guido Ferracio in February 1948. In the photograph Peter relaxes by taking a swing with a golf club.

Lord Gordon Macdonald of Gwaenysgor (1888-1966) was the son of Thomas and Ellen Macdonald of Ashton-in-Makerfield. Born at Gwaenysgor, Prestatyn, he began his working life as a pit boy when 13 years of age, earning 10s per week at Bryn Colliery. Subsequently he became a coal hewer. He was educated at St Luke's Elementary School, Stubshaw Cross, before moving on to Ruskin College, Oxford. During the 1921 mining stoppage he served in the County Wages Board as a Member of the Executive Council of the Miners' Federation of Great Britain. In 1929, after Stephen Walsh resigned as MP of Ince, Gordon Macdonald became the automatic choice. In June 1929 he was returned with a majority of 16,831. By 1942 he was offered and accepted the post of Regimental Controller of Lancashire, Cheshire and Northern Wales. Four years later he took up the post of Governor of Newfoundland where he went with his wife and youngest daughter Glenys. His terms of reference were to persuade Newfoundland politicians to join with Canada, a mission which was successful. In 1949 he returned to England where he was appointed Postmaster General and after the fall of the Attlee government in 1951, he was appointed National Governor of the BBC for Wales, a post for which he was well suited as he had a perfect command of the Welsh language. Macdonald was a leading Congregationalist, teetotaller and non-smoker. He also supported Wigan Rugby Club. He was married to Mary Lewis of Blaenau Festiniog.

In March 1983, Joe Gormley (1917–93), the former miners' leader, returned to his home town of Ashton-in-Makerfield to officially attend the commencement of work on the site of the Prudential Development. The £2 million industrial complex is now known as the South Lancs Industrial Estate. To mark the occasion Joe buried a time capsule with help from children of his old school of St Oswald's. The capsule contained local newspapers and other artefacts including a tape recording of carols sung by children from St Oswald's. Born at Ashton, Joe was educated at the local Roman Catholic school before being employed in the mining industry. He served as a local councillor before being elected to the National Executive Committee of the NUM in 1957. He became General Secretary of the North West Area in 1961. Later he was appointed President of the NUM, remaining in office from 1971 to 1982. A former member of the TUC General Council between 1973 and 1980, he died on 27 May 1993. In 1969 he was awarded an OBE and in 1992 became a Life Peer, taking the title of Baron Gormley.

Workmen demolishing Golborne South station in the early 1960s.

Acknowledgements

The author is grateful to the following for allowing photographs in this book to be reproduced: Bert Worsley, Ronnie Marsh, the Golborne Local History Society, Jim Fairhurst, Mrs J. Fleming, Mrs Calderbank, Mr Higgins, Mr Parkinson, the minister of Park Lane Unitarian church and others.

Thanks also to Alastair Gillies, Heritage Services Manager, for suggesting this project, Len Hudson of the Heritage Services for producing the photographs, Nicholas Webb, Archives Officer, for his valued advice and assistance, Bob Blakeman, Education and Outreach Manager at Wigan History Shop for all his help and advice with regard to the final presentation, and to Stephanie Tsang and Barbara Miller, who did the typing.